W9-ASU-781

This book belongs to

_____

Favorite Tales from
Grimm

A Treasured Collection

———•———

Retold by KIT SCHORSCH
Illustrated by KITTY DIAMANTES
Cover design by SHANNON OSBORNE THOMPSON

DALMATIAN PRESS

For Booby with Love
—K.S.

To M. R. and D. R. Serafy
—K.D.

From earliest times, people have gathered around the storyteller, and though no one knows exactly where or how fairy tales first started, in all parts of the world they share similar themes. Fairy tales give form to the desires and fears of all people and reflect a strong faith in justice. Evil is punished and goodness is rewarded.

Simple yet rich in detail, the tales were woven like the cloth woven in every village. The pattern remained constant while embellishments varied with telling and time. In a world where belongings were few, these tales became treasured possessions.

At the beginning of the nineteenth century, when Germany was still a land of kingdoms and fair princesses, Jakob and Wilhelm Grimm set out to find the storytellers and record the old tales. For the first time, the spirit and simplicity of this oral tradition made its appearance in recorded literature, and it wasn't long before Rumpelstiltskin, Sleeping Beauty, Hansel, Gretel, and Little Red Riding Hood could be found wandering through the pages of the storybooks of many lands.

Favorite Tales from Grimm gathers some of the storytellers' most enchanting tales in one large, lavishly illustrated book. Children will be greeted by the timeless magic that has put Grimms' fairy tales among some of the most universally beloved stories in literature.

ALL ART AND EDITORIAL MATERIAL IS OWNED BY DALMATIAN PRESS.
ISBN: 1-57759-421-5

FIRST PUBLISHED IN THE UNITED STATES IN 2000 BY DALMATIAN PRESS, USA

COPYRIGHT © 2000 DALMATIAN PRESS
PRINTED AND BOUND IN THE USA

THE DALMATIAN PRESS NAME, LOGO AND SPOTTED SPINE ARE
TRADEMARKS OF DALMATIAN PRESS, FRANKLIN, TENNESSEE 37067.

ALL RIGHTS RESERVED. WRITTEN PERMISSION MUST BE SECURED FROM THE PUBLISHER TO USE OR
REPRODUCE ANY PART OF THIS BOOK, EXCEPT FOR BRIEF QUOTATIONS IN CRITICAL REVIEWS OR PUBLICITY.

11151a

00 01 02 QWK 10 9 8 7 6 5 4 3 2 1

Contents

The Frog Prince

A long time ago there lived a king who had three beautiful daughters. The youngest of the three was so beautiful that the sun itself, who had seen so much in this world, was amazed at her beauty. Near the king's castle was a great forest, and it was here that the youngest daughter liked to play. Often the princess would go and sit by an old well under a large lime tree and play with her favorite toy, a golden ball. She loved to throw the ball into the air and catch it.

One day, when the princess was playing happily with her ball, she accidentally dropped it into the well. The princess peered into the well to see if she could get the ball back, but it had disappeared beneath the water. She began to cry bitterly, for she knew that her favorite toy was lost.

Suddenly she heard a voice. "Why do you cry, little princess? Your sobbing is so sad that soon the whole forest will become sad if you do not stop."

The princess looked around to see who had spoken. There, sitting on the edge of the well, was an ugly, slimy green frog.

"I am weeping because my ball has fallen into the well," she said.

"Don't cry," said the frog. "I can help you. But tell me, Your Highness, what will you give me if I bring your ball back to you?"

"Anything your heart desires," she said. "My beautiful jewels, or my fine clothes—why, even this little gold crown I am wearing."

"I do not want jewels or clothes," said the frog. "But if you will love me as your friend and let me stay with you as your companion—if you will let me play with you and sit with you at the table and eat from your plate, and sleep with you in your bed—if you will promise me all of this, I will bring you back your golden ball."

"Yes, yes," said the little princess happily, "all this I will promise." But the princess thought to herself: "What a silly frog. He plays in the well with other frogs and toads. He is not fit to be a companion to a princess."

As soon as the frog heard the princess's promise he dived into the well, found the ball, brought it back up. The king's daughter picked up her ball, smiled gratefully at the frog, and ran quickly home to the castle.

"Wait, wait!" called the frog. "I cannot run as fast as you. Take me with you!" But the frog's calling and croaking was of no use. The princess was not listening, and as soon as she was home again she forgot about her promise.

The next day, while the princess was eating dinner with the king, they heard a noise on the marble staircase—a strange, slippery slap-slap noise. This was soon followed by a loud knock on the door. Then a voice said, "Little princess, please open this big door for me."

The princess ran to the door to see who was there, and whom should she see but the ugly, slimy green frog. She slammed the door quickly and went back to her seat.

The king could tell that his daughter was frightened. "My dear," he said, "who was at the door that has scared you so? Perhaps a terrible giant or a goblin, whom you fear will take you away?"

"No," said the child, "much worse than a giant or a goblin! An ugly, slimy frog!"

"And what did he want?" asked the king.

"Oh, Father," she cried, "yesterday when I was playing in the forest my golden ball dropped into the well. Because this frog brought it back to me, I promised that he could be my companion and friend. But I never thought he would leave the forest. I do not want a *frog* as a friend."

"You have made a promise," said the king, "and you must keep it."

So the princess opened the door, and the frog hopped behind her, back to the table where she was still eating her dinner. Then the frog asked the princess to pick him up and put him on the table so he could eat dinner with her. The princess did not want to do this, but the king looked sternly at his daughter and reminded her of her promise. So she obeyed her father and lifted the frog onto the table.

The princess offered the frog some soup, so he hopped right into her bowl and ate it all up! The princess did not like this at all. She was not happy sharing her food with the frog, but the frog loved what he ate and was very happy to be with the princess.

After dinner the frog said, "Now I am tired. Please carry me to your room so we may go to sleep."

The princess started to cry. She did not want to share her soft, warm bed with the ugly, slimy green frog. The king became angry with his daughter. "It is not right that you neglect a friend who has helped you in your need," he said. "Now you must repay his kindness."

Reluctantly the princess lifted up the frog and carried him to her room. But since her father wasn't there to see, she left him in a dark corner.

The frog was cold there, and said, "I want to sleep as you do. Put me in your bed." The princess was now tired and angry. She picked up the frog, but instead of putting him in her bed she threw him with all her might against the wall. "Now be quiet!" she cried furiously.

As the frog touched the wall he instantly changed into the most handsome prince the princess had ever seen!

"Thank you," the prince said. "You have broken the spell a terrible witch cast upon me. Only a princess could break it. If your father the king is willing," he said, "tomorrow we will leave together for my kingdom and be married without delay."

The next morning was warm and bright. The king happily gave his approval to the marriage. The prince and princess set off at once in a beautiful carriage pulled by eight white horses harnessed together with shining golden chains. As they rode away together bells rang throughout the land. And the prince and princess lived happily together ever after.

Mother Holle

There was once a widow with two daughters: one pretty and clever, the other ugly and lazy. The woman preferred the ugly one because she was her own child, whereas the pretty girl was really her stepchild. The woman made her stepdaughter do all the work. The poor child was also forced to sit by the well and spin when all her other work was done. Her fingers became so sore they would often bleed.

One day while she was spinning, a drop of blood fell on her spindle, so the girl leaned over the well to clean it off. But as she did this the spindle slipped from her hand and fell to the bottom of the well and disappeared from sight.

The young girl ran and told her stepmother, who said, "You stupid girl! Jump down into the well and get it!" The poor girl was very frightened, but did as she was told. As she jumped into the well she fainted.

When she awoke, she found herself lying in a beautiful meadow covered with thousands of pretty flowers. The girl did not know where she was, so she stood up and began to walk through this strange and beautiful place. She had not gone far when she came to an oven full of bread. "Take us out! Take us out!" the bread called. "Or we will be burned to a crisp!" The girl quickly opened the oven door and carefully removed each loaf of bread. When that was done, she walked on and soon came to a large apple tree covered with fine ripe fruit. "Shake me! Shake me!" cried the tree. "For my apples are all ripe!" So the girl shook the tree until every apple fell off. She collected all the apples and put them in a neat pile. Then she went on her way.

Before long the girl came to a little house. There an old woman sat at the doorstep. "Come and live with me," said the old woman, "and you can be my helper. If you do my work as I ask, I will reward you well. But you must always make my bed properly. You must take care to shake it until all the feathers fly. Then everyone in the world below will say that it is snowing. You may call me Mother Holle."

The young girl agreed to stay with the old woman, for she did not know where else she could live. She worked very hard.

And every day she always shook out Mother Holle's bed until all the feathers flew. The old woman was very kind to the girl; she never scolded and they ate good food. The girl was very comfortable, but after she had lived with Mother Holle for some time she became homesick, and said to Mother Holle: "I know that my life is much better here with you than it was before, but I miss my family and I wish to go home."

Mother Holle was sad to hear these words, but replied, "It is right that you should want to go. And since you have served me so well, I will show you the way back to the world myself."

So Mother Holle took the girl by the hand and led her to an open door. There she bade the girl good-bye. As the young girl walked through the door a shower of gold fell upon her and covered her from head to toe. "That is your reward for being such a good girl," said Mother Holle. Then she gave her back the spindle that had fallen into the well, and sent her on her way.

Soon the young girl found herself once again in her own land, not far from home. When she walked into her own barnyard, the hen called out:

"Cluck, click, clack!
The golden maid's come back!"

The stepmother heard the hen's call and ran out of the house. Seeing the girl covered with gold, the stepmother welcomed her. The girl told her

stepmother all that had happened. The mother wanted the same good fortune for her own ugly and lazy daughter. The next day she sent her own child out to spin by the well. The lazy girl didn't want to spin, so she pricked her finger with a thorn, then rubbed the blood on the spindle and threw it down the well. At once she jumped down after it. The lazy sister came to the same beautiful meadow that her sister had found herself in, and she followed the same path. When she came to the oven the bread again called: "Take us out! Take us out! Or we will be burned to a crisp!"

"Tut!" said the ugly girl. "Do you think I would make myself dirty just to help you?"

She walked on and soon came to the apple tree. "Shake me! Shake me!" it cried. "For my apples are all ripe!"

"Bah!" said the lazy girl. "Suppose an apple should drop on my head and hurt me!" And she went on her way.

When she came to Mother Holle's house, the old woman asked the lazy girl to be her maid. At once the girl agreed, and Mother Holle took her in. She explained all that the girl was to do. On the first day the girl worked very hard. But on the second day she became lazy, and on the third day she wouldn't even get out of bed! She didn't make Mother Holle's bed as she had been told, and the feathers never flew. So it wasn't long before Mother Holle was dissatisfied and asked the lazy girl to leave. The lazy girl didn't mind this. She was very happy to go, and thought to herself: "Now I'll get my shower of gold."

Mother Holle led the lazy girl to the same door to which she had led her sister. But as the girl passed through it, instead of gold a shower of pitch fell on the child. "This is your reward for being so lazy!" said the old woman, and she closed the door behind her.

When the lazy girl got home, the hen cried:

> "Cluck, click, clack!
> Our lazy girl's come back!"

The pitch stuck to the lazy girl for the rest of her life, because she was too lazy to rub it off.

The Elves and the Shoemaker

There was once a shoemaker who had become so poor that at last he found he had enough leather left to make only one pair of shoes. So he cut out the leather for the shoes he would make the next day, and after saying his prayers, he went to bed.

In the morning he went down to his shop to begin work, and there on the worktable, where the night before he had left the cut leather, was the most beautiful pair of shoes. Every stitch was perfect. He had never seen such fine work. He thought they were far more beautiful than any shoes he could ever make.

That very day a man came into the shop and was so delighted with the shoes that he bought them at once, and even paid more for them than the shoemaker had asked. With this money the shoemaker went out and bought enough leather to make two more pairs of shoes.

That evening the shoemaker again carefully cut the leather and laid it out ready for the next day. Then he said his prayers and went to bed.

When the shoemaker came down the next morning, he again found that his work was already done. There on his worktable, where he had left only the cut leather the night before, were two new pairs of shoes, both as beautiful as the first pair. The shoemaker had no trouble selling these shoes, and once again he was paid more money than he had asked. With the money

he bought leather for four pairs of shoes. The same wonderful thing happened the next day, and the next and the next. Whatever leather the shoemaker cut at night he found as finished shoes the next morning. Soon the shoemaker became quite rich.

Now, one day, as Christmas was approaching, the shoemaker said to his wife, "Why don't we try to find out who is helping us to finish all our shoes?" His wife liked the idea, so that night, after cutting out the leather, they hid themselves in a dark corner of the workshop.

When midnight came, two naked little elves came in, sat down at the worktable, and at once set to work on the shoes. The shoemaker could hardly believe his eyes. With their little hands they hammered and stitched and sewed and did the most wonderful work. In no time at all they were finished. Then they quickly and quietly hurried away.

The next morning the shoemaker's wife said, "These little elves have changed our fortune. They must be very cold without any clothes. I will make them little shirts and little vests, and coats and pants and little hats. I'll even knit them little stockings. And you must make them little shoes."

The shoemaker agreed, and said, "They have done so much for us. It would be nice to do something for them."

So the shoemaker and his wife spent all day working, and when night came they laid out all the little presents on the worktable and went to hide in the corner. As midnight struck the elves came in. They were very surprised to find no work laid out for them to do. But when they saw all the little clothes laid out instead, how they danced and laughed! There were never such happy little elves. They put on their beautiful new clothes and began to sing:

"Now we're such a pretty sight,
Why should we work all night?"

They danced all over the room — under the table, on top of the bench — and then right out the door. The elves never came back, but from that time on the shoemaker always prospered and was never poor again.

Sleeping Beauty

Once upon a time there lived a king and queen who had all the riches in the world except that which is most precious: a child. This made them very sad, for a child was all they desired. One day, when the queen was walking by a river, a little fish stuck its head out of the water and said: "Very soon, my queen, your dearest wish will come true, for you shall have a daughter." And the fish disappeared immediately.

Before long, as the fish had predicted, the queen gave birth to a beautiful baby girl. This lovely child was the king's greatest joy, and to celebrate her birth he called all his ministers and announced that he would hold a great feast. To this feast the king and queen invited not just family, friends, and neighbors, but also the fairies who lived throughout the land. In this kingdom there were thirteen fairies, but the king had only twelve golden plates on which they could eat, so he decided that one of the fairies would not be invited. The great feast was held, and as it came to an end and the fairies were preparing to leave, each came forward to bestow a special gift on the little princess. One brought her virtue, another beauty, another wisdom,

another riches, and so on, until the child had all that was fine in the world. But suddenly, after the eleventh fairy had blessed the child with her gift, the thirteenth fairy, who was angry because she had not been invited, appeared at the door.

"Your gifts will all be wasted," she said, "for I decree that in the princess's fifteenth year she will prick her finger on a spindle and instantly drop down dead." Everyone gasped in horror, but before another word could be said, the thirteenth fairy was gone.

Luckily, the twelfth fairy had not as yet given the child her gift. She came forward and said, "Although I cannot undo the thirteenth fairy's curse, I can soften it. The prick from the spindle shall not kill the princess, but only put her into a gentle slumber for one hundred years."

The king, who hoped to save his child from the evil that the thirteenth fairy had foretold, at once ordered that every spindle in the kingdom be destroyed. As the princess grew, all the good fairies' blessings came to be, for she was beautiful, virtuous, and wise, and everyone who knew her loved her.

On the day of the princess's fifteenth birthday, it so happened that the king and queen were away. The princess was happily wandering alone through parts of the castle she had never before explored: hidden chambers and out-of-the-way rooms. At last she came to a small tower, and after climbing a winding stairway, she arrived at a little door. In the door was a rusty key, and when she turned it the door swung open, revealing a small room. Inside the room an old, old woman sat spinning. The princess had never before seen a spindle, for they had long been banished from the castle, and so she asked the woman: "Old lady, please tell me what it is that you are doing there."

"I am spinning, dear child," said the woman, who continued busily at her work.

The princess asked the old woman if she could try it herself. No sooner had the princess taken the spindle into her hand than she pricked her finger and fell down lifeless.

But she was not dead—she had only fallen into a deep sleep. Just then, the king and queen arrived back at their castle, and they too fell into a deep sleep. And with them all their kingdom fell asleep as well — the horses in their stables and the dogs in their kennels, the pigeons on the rooftops, and even the small flies on the walls. All the fires in the hearths stopped blazing and slept; and the meat that was roasting stood still; and the maid about to pluck her chicken, and even the cook who was about to pull at the kitchen boy's hair for spilling some soup—they all fell asleep where they stood. Everything in the castle stopped and slept soundly.

As the years went by a thick hedge of thorns grew around the castle, and with each passing year, as the castle slept, the hedge grew higher and thicker, until at last the castle was completely hidden from the world outside. But word went forth throughout the land that within the castle slept a princess so beautiful that she became known to all as Sleeping Beauty.

Many a king's son tried to break through the hedge of thorns to find her, but the hedge was so thick, and the thorns so sharp, that every prince who tried to get through became trapped by the brambles and died.

Many years passed, and many princes were caught by the brambles as they tried to get to the princess. At last, most people forgot all about the hidden castle. Then one day a king's son came into the land and happened to meet an old man who told him the story of the hidden castle in which the beautiful Sleeping Beauty lay. The prince wanted to find the castle at once. But the old man warned the young prince that he had heard from his grandfather that many princes had died trying to reach the princess. He warned the prince not to go.

"Nothing can deter me," said the prince. "I will go and find Sleeping Beauty."

It so happened that that very day was the day when the hundred-year spell was to end, so when the prince approached the castle he found no brambles, only beautiful flowering shrubs and bushes, for the thorn hedge had changed and all was a luscious green. He passed through all of it with no difficulty. When the prince arrived at the castle he was very surprised to find the whole court asleep, with everything exactly as it had been for a hundred years: the horses still stood in their stables and the dogs were motionless in their kennels, the pigeons asleep on the rooftops and the flies on the walls. And the maid in her sleep was still about to pluck her chicken, and even the cook was about to pull the kitchen boy's hair.

The prince wandered through the castle, where all was quiet and still except for the sound of his own breathing. At last he came to a tower. Step by step he climbed to the top, and in the little room he found Sleeping Beauty just as she had fallen. She was so beautiful that the prince could not take his eyes from her. He bent down to kiss her, and at that very moment the spell was broken. Sleeping Beauty awoke and looked at the prince in wonder. He told her that she and the whole castle had been asleep and explained to her all that had happened. Then they left the tower together and went into the court, where all was now as it had been a hundred years before. Sleeping Beauty found her parents, who had just woken up as well, and they looked around in wonder. The horses were awake and shaking themselves, and the dogs jumped and ran happily, and the pigeons flew from the rooftops and gracefully soared over the land. And the flies started to buzz merrily and the fires started once again to blaze and the meat started once again to cook and the maid started at last to pluck her chicken and the cook finally pulled the kitchen boy's hair. There was much activity and much excitement because the whole castle was awake and getting ready for a great feast, for there was to be a wedding. The prince had asked Sleeping Beauty to marry him, and she had happily said yes. The celebration lasted for many months and the prince and Sleeping Beauty lived happily ever after.

The Fisherman and His Wife

A very long time ago in a small hut by the sea there lived a poor fisherman and his wife. Each day passed exactly as the one before it: as soon as the sun came up the fisherman went and sat by the sea and fished, but he caught little. All day he watched the changing tides of the sea and the changing colors of the sky. In the evening, as the sun went down, he would go home to his wife.

One day, when the fisherman pulled in his line, he found he had caught a very large flounder. He was delighted, but before he had time to admire his catch the flounder started to talk. ''I am not really a flounder,'' said the fish. ''I am an enchanted prince. Please throw me back into the sea. If you kill me it will not help you. You will only eat me and after a few mouthfuls I will be gone. And I don't even taste very good. Be kind and let me swim away free.''

''You need not worry,'' said the fisherman. ''I would be a fool to eat a talking flounder. I will gladly set you free.'' So he carefully unhooked the flounder and dropped him back into the water. He swam away at once and the fisherman went home to his wife.

''Did you catch anything today?'' she asked, as she always did.

''Yes,'' he said, ''I caught a talking flounder who said he was an enchanted prince, so I put him back into the water and let him swim free.''

''Did you not ask him for a wish?'' asked the wife.

''No,'' said the man. ''There is nothing that I wish for.''

''Well, I have a wish,'' said the woman. ''Do you think I want to spend my life in this little hut? I want to live in a beautiful cottage. Go back to the sea and call the talking flounder. Tell him we wish for a cottage. I am sure he will give you whatever you want. You saved his life.''

So the man went back to the sea to call the flounder. He was not very happy to do this, but he wished to please his wife. He thought there was nothing wrong with their little hut.

When the fisherman got to the sea it was no longer shining and brilliantly blue. It had turned a dark green that was not very pretty. A storm was brewing. The fisherman stood near the water's edge and called:

"Talking flounder deep in the sea, once caught, I set you free.
Come, I call for my wife, Ilsebel, she has a wish that I must tell."

Immediately the flounder appeared. "What is your wife's wish?" he asked.

"My wife says I should not have let you go without first making a wish. She does not want to live in a hut. She wishes instead for a cottage."

"Go home," said the flounder. "You will find that she has her wish."

So the man went home and found his wife sitting outside a pretty little cottage. "Come, look at our new home," she said, taking his hand. What a change from their old hut! There was a bright entrance hall, a sitting room with cozy sofas, a pretty little kitchen, and a bedroom with a big bed. Outside in the yard were chickens and ducks. There was also a small garden

filled with vegetables and ripe fruit trees.

"Isn't this better than our tiny hut?" asked the wife.

"It is nice," admitted the fisherman. "We can live here happily for the rest of our lives."

"Maybe . . ." said the wife. Then they ate their supper and went to bed.

It was only a week later when the wife said to her husband, "This cottage is too small. The flounder should have given us a better home. Go and tell him I wish instead for a stone castle."

"But our new cottage is nice," said the fisherman. "And we do not need a castle."

"A castle would be much better than this little cottage. You saved the flounder's life. He can certainly give us a castle."

"But he gave us our wish. I do not like asking for more," said the fisherman.

"Don't be a fool," said his wife. "Go and ask."

So the man went. This time the sea was even darker and less clear than before, and the sky was darker too. But the fisherman called out:

"Talking flounder deep in the sea, once caught, I set you free.
    Come, I call for my wife, Ilsebel, she has a wish that I must tell."

"What is it your wife now wishes for?" asked the flounder. The fisherman was very embarrassed. "A stone castle," he said.

"Go home," said the flounder. "You will find that she has her wish."

The fisherman went home and where the cottage had stood just one hour earlier, there was now an enormous stone castle with grand steps leading up to it. His wife was on the steps, and she reached out her hand to him. "Come inside and I will show you our new home," she said happily.

What a home! There was a grand entrance hall of marble and servants who opened wide the large doors as they walked from room to room. In each room they found elegant furniture and soft plush carpets. The walls were covered with beautiful tapestries, and crystal chandeliers hung from the ceilings. It was everything the wife had imagined a castle to be. Horses in clean stables and a coach house filled with fancy coaches were outside. There was also a beautiful garden of flowers and fruit trees, and in the land around the castle were deer and rabbits and many other animals.

"Isn't this better than the cottage?" asked the wife after she had shown the fisherman everything.

"It is very nice," said the fisherman. "We can live here contented for the rest of our lives."

"Maybe . . ." said the wife, and after they ate the fine supper that had been prepared for them, they climbed into soft feather beds and went to sleep.

The next morning when the wife awoke she gazed out the window at the beautiful countryside. Her husband was still asleep, so she nudged him impatiently. "Wake up," she said, "there is much to do today. Do you see all this? It all could be ours. We could rule all this land. I want you to go tell the flounder that you wish to be king."

"Why?" asked the fisherman. "This castle is very nice and I do not want to be king."

"If you do not want to be king, then *I* will be king. Go tell the flounder that is my wish."

"But I can't ask the flounder to make you king. He has already given us this magnificent castle."

"What is this castle?" she said. "Why should I live here when I can be king? It will be no problem for the flounder. Go and ask him at once."

Reluctantly the fisherman went back to the sea. Now the water was dark gray, the waves were raging, and the sky was more stormy than before. But once again the fisherman called out:

"Talking flounder deep in the sea, once caught, I set you free.
Come, I call for my wife, Ilsebel, she has a wish that I must tell."

"What is it your wife now wishes for?" asked the flounder.

"I do not ask this happily, Flounder. Now her wish is to be king."

"Go home," said the flounder. "You will find that she has her wish."

And when the fisherman arrived back where the stone castle had stood earlier that day, there was now an enormous royal castle. At each corner was a great tower, and a sentinel stood at the huge main gate. Soldiers in uniforms of red, white, and black stood at different posts. Inside, the fisherman found enormous stairways and halls of pink marble and all the rooms were decorated with majestic marble statues. There were thick curtains and gold-laced tapestries and more elegance than the fisherman had ever imagined. At last he was led into an enormous hall with windows higher than two men. In the center of the room sat his wife on a magnificent gold throne, wearing a beautiful gown and a crown of gold and diamonds. All around her stood courtiers waiting to serve her.

"Well," said the fisherman, "now you are king."

"Yes," said his wife. "Isn't this better than a simple stone castle? Look at all my courtiers! Look at the splendor of our new home!"

"It is magnificent," agreed her husband. "Be contented with this. You have what you wished for. We have need for nothing greater."

"But," said his wife, "I wish for more. What is a king when I can be emperor? Go to the flounder at once. Tell him I wish to be emperor."

"Surely you can be happy with all this," said the fisherman. "I do not want to ask the flounder to make you emperor. There is only one emperor in the entire land. I'm sure the flounder cannot do this."

"If he can make me king, he can make me emperor," said the wife. "Do not disobey me. Remember I am now the king! Go at once!"

So reluctantly the fisherman went down to the sea, but as he went he thought about his wife's wish, and he thought it was too much. And when he arrived, the sea was almost black and very stormy, and the waves were very big and looked dangerous. The sky was somber. But even though the fisherman was frightened he called out:

"Talking flounder deep in the sea, once caught, I set you free.
Come, I call for my wife, Ilsebel, she has a wish that I must tell."

"What is it she now wishes for?" asked the flounder.

The fisherman was very nervous. "My wife wishes to be emperor," he said softly.

"Go home," said the flounder. "You will find that she has her wish."

When he got back to the place where the royal castle had stood only a few hours earlier, the fisherman now saw an enormous palace. It was made of polished marble inlaid with colored jewels. Gold statues adorned the halls so that the whole building sparkled and glistened in the sun. Everywhere around the castle there were not just soldiers, but barons and counts and dukes of the land. All were there only to serve the emperor. The fisherman was taken to a splendid room in an inner court and there sat his wife on a throne even bigger than the last. Her gown was even more wonderful than before. It was encrusted with gems, as were her crown, her scepter, and her orb. Around her were many noblemen and gentlewomen waiting to talk to her, but the fisherman went right up to her and said, ''Well, now you are emperor.''

''Yes,'' said his wife. ''Isn't it much better than merely being king?'' The fisherman stood back a few feet and gazed at his wife and all the beautiful things around her. ''At last you can be contented,'' he said.

The emperor looked at her husband. ''Do not just stand there,'' she said. ''I may be emperor, but now I want to be Pope. Go immediately and tell the flounder of my wish.''

''No, wife,'' the fisherman said. ''I cannot ask the flounder this. There is only one Pope in all of Christendom. The flounder cannot change that. You have many great things and there is no reason to wish for more.''

"I will be Pope. If the flounder can make me emperor, he can make me Pope. Go at once. I am the emperor and this is my command."

And so the fisherman set off, though he was miserable as he went. He did not want to tell the flounder of his wife's wish to be Pope, because he thought this would certainly be more than the flounder would do. And as he went toward the sea, the sky turned black, the clouds moved very quickly, and the wind became very fierce. When he got there the water was very rough and tempestuous with foam blowing everywhere. It was clear that the worst storm imaginable was brewing. But the fisherman had to obey his wife, the emperor, so he went to the water and called once again:

"Talking flounder deep in the sea, once caught, I set you free.
 Come, I call for my wife, Ilsebel, she has a wish that I must tell."

As before, the flounder appeared immediately. "What is it your wife now wishes for?" he asked.

The fisherman shook with fear. "Alas, flounder, although I am not happy telling you this, her wish is to be Pope."

"Go home," said the flounder. "You will find that she has her wish."

So home again went the fisherman. And where only an hour before had stood the emperor's palace, the fisherman now found an enormous cathedral surrounded by a variety of palaces. The fisherman was led inside this majestic

complex where all the fine stone and marble glistened with thousands of white candles and elaborate gold ornaments. At last he arrived at an inner sanctuary where he found his wife sitting on a papal throne dressed in pure white. Kneeling before her were dignitaries from many lands.

"Well," said the fisherman, "you are now Pope?"

"Yes," she said, "I am Pope." And the fisherman stood and looked around in amazement, for he had never seen nor could have imagined so much beauty and so many riches.

Then he said, "Be contented with this, wife. There is nothing more you can wish for."

"I will see," said his wife firmly.

But the woman was not content and did not sleep that night, for her greed was so great that she lay awake tossing and turning trying to think of what else she could possibly wish for. She felt sure the flounder would give her whatever she wanted, but she could not think of anything.

The next morning, when the sun and the pink of early morning started to spread across the land, the Pope went to the window to watch the sun awaken all. Suddenly she thought to herself: "Why can't *I* make the sun rise and all the world rise with it? If I could do this, I would truly have all." She quickly went to wake the fisherman.

"Husband," she said, shaking him roughly. "Go at once to the flounder. Tell him that I wish to control the sun and all the earth—I wish to be God!"

The fisherman thought he must be dreaming, because he did not believe that his wife thought the flounder could make her God. But the wife shook him again. "Up! Up! Get up! Go at once to the flounder! I shall never be content until I have these powers too."

The husband turned pale. "No," he said. "This the flounder cannot do. He made you king and then emperor and now he has even made you Pope. But he cannot make you God. Be contented with what you have. Please, wife, be contented at last."

But the wife flew into a wild rage. She screamed and stamped her feet. Her hair flew all around so that she looked like a woman gone mad. *"No, no, no!"* she yelled. *"I will be God and the flounder must give me my wish! I must be God or I will never be content. Go at once!"* she bellowed.

The fisherman was terrified. He had never before seen his wife in such a

34

state. He dressed hurriedly and ran to the sea as quickly as he could.

When he got to the sea there was a storm raging so fiercely that going near the water was very dangerous. The waves were wild and high. The wind blew so strongly that houses, trees, animals, and even people were blown about and rocks tumbled from the mountains. The sky was pitch black with lightning and thunder cracking down again and again into the roaring sea. But the fisherman summoned all his courage and called:

> "Talking flounder deep in the sea, once caught, I set you free.
> Come, I call for my wife, Ilsebel, she has a wish that I must tell."

Immediately, as before, the flounder appeared. "What is it your wife now wishes for?" he asked.

"I truly do not want to tell you," said the fisherman, "but I must. Alas, she wishes to be God."

"Go home," said the fish. "You will find she does not have her wish."

And the fisherman went home, back to the same spot where the Pope's residence had been just hours earlier, and just hours before that the emperor's palace, and hours before that the king's castle, and before that the stone castle, and before that the pretty little cottage, and before that their own humble hut. And there the fisherman found his wife, just as she had always been before he caught the talking flounder, stooped over her little fire. And as it had always been, she had nothing much to say, and they lived the rest of their days just that way.

Little Red Riding Hood

Once upon a time on the other side of the woods there lived a little girl who was dearly loved by all. She was her grandmother's favorite, and the old woman would give her beloved grandchild anything just to see her smile. One very special time, she gave her grandchild a riding hood made of beautiful red velvet. The girl loved her hood so much that she wore it everywhere she went. Before long, everyone called the girl Little Red Riding Hood.

One day Little Red Riding Hood's grandmother became ill, so her mother said to her: "Take this cake and bottle of wine and these other good things to eat to your grandmother. They will make her feel much better. Go through the woods, but be sure to stay on the path. Take care, and do not stop to talk to anyone."

"I will be very careful," Little Red Riding Hood promised her mother as she kissed her good-bye.

As Little Red Riding Hood was skipping through the woods, she met a wolf. But Little Red Riding Hood wasn't afraid, because she had never met a wolf before.

"Good morning, Little Red Riding Hood," said the wolf. "Where are you going this bright sunny day?"

"I'm off to visit my grandmother, who is ill and lives on the other side of the woods," she replied.

"And what do you have in your basket?" asked the wolf, who was feeling very hungry.

"I have cake and wine to make my grandmother feel better," said Little Red Riding Hood.

Then the wolf thought: "My, I am so hungry. How tasty this little girl would be. I would like to eat her grandmother too. If I am clever, I can eat both of them!" Then with a sneaky smile he said to her, "Little Red Riding

Hood, since it is still so early, why don't you come with me and look at the pretty flowers that grow in the woods? You will still have plenty of time to get to your grandmother's."

But Little Red Riding Hood remembered what her mother had said, so she shook her head. "My mother told me not to wander off the path," she replied.

"But why not pick some flowers for your grandmother?" asked the wolf. "I'm sure they would make her feel much better."

"I think maybe that would be all right," said Little Red Riding Hood. "Flowers are so cheerful. Surely they will help to make my grandmother well. And I won't have to go very far off the path."

So Little Red Riding Hood went to pick some flowers while the wolf ran ahead to the grandmother's house. When he got there he knocked on the door.

"Who's there?" called the grandmother.

"Little Red Riding Hood," said the wolf, making his voice as much like Little Red Riding Hood's as he could. "I have brought cake and wine to make you feel better."

"Lift the latch and come in," the grandmother said, "for I am too weak, my dear, to get out of bed."

The wolf opened the door and ran to the grandmother's bed. Before she could blink the wolf opened his great big mouth and swallowed her whole in one gulp. Then he put on the grandmother's nightgown and cap, tucked himself into her bed, and pulled the bedclothes right up to his nose. The wolf did not have long to wait before Little Red Riding Hood arrived at the cottage. She knocked at the door.

"Who's there?" called the wolf in a soft voice, for he was trying to sound like the grandmother.

"It's Little Red Riding Hood, and I've come to visit," she said.

"Lift the latch, open the door, and come in, my dear," said the wolf, "for I am too weak to leave my bed."

When Little Red Riding Hood saw her grandmother, she thought she looked very strange indeed.

"Grandmother," she said, "what big ears you have!"

"All the better to hear you with, my dear," said the wolf, and he pulled the bedclothes up a little higher.

"Grandmother, what great big eyes you have!" said Little Red Riding Hood.

"All the better to see you with, my dear," replied the wolf.

"Grandmother, what great big hands you have!" said Little Red Riding Hood.

"All the better to hug you with, my dear," said the wolf.

"Grandmother, what great big teeth you have!" said Little Red Riding Hood.

"All the better to eat you with!" cried the wolf, and with that he jumped out of bed, grabbed Little Red Riding Hood with his great big hands, and swallowed her whole.

Since the wolf was now very full, he became sleepy. So he closed his

eyes, and before long was fast asleep, snoring loudly. A hunter who was passing by heard the noise. "My," he said, "the old woman is snoring very noisily. I wonder if something is the matter."

He went inside the cottage and found the wolf fast asleep. The hunter said to himself: "Here is that mischievous wolf I've been looking for. Finally I have found him!" He was about to slay the wolf with his axe when he thought to himself: "First I will cut open the wolf, just in case there's anyone inside." So while the wolf was still asleep, the hunter cut open his stomach. He had cut just a tiny bit, when he saw a little red hood, and then out popped Little Red Riding Hood. "Oh, how scared I was!" she cried. "It is so dark inside the wolf!" Then the hunter cut some more, and out came the grandmother. She was still alive, but felt very stiff. "How cramped it is inside the wolf," she said. She was very happy to see Little Red Riding Hood.

Little Red Riding Hood quickly ran to get some big stones, which the huntsman put into the wolf's belly. Grandmother took a needle and thread and carefully sewed him up. When the wolf awoke, he was too heavy to run away, and after taking one step he dropped down dead.

The huntsman skinned the wolf for his beautiful fur and took it home. The grandmother ate her cake and wine and felt much, much better. Little Red Riding Hood gave her grandmother a kiss and said, "I will never again leave the path to run in the woods, and I will always remember to listen to what my mother tells me!"

Spindle, Shuttle, and Needle

Once a very long time ago, there was a poor little girl whose mother and father had both died when she was a tiny baby. So she was sent to live with her godmother in a small cottage at the edge of a small town. This old woman made her living by spinning, weaving, and sewing. She was very kind to the little girl. She loved her dearly, and brought her up well. She taught her all she knew.

When the girl was fifteen, her godmother became very ill and told her: "It will not be long before I die. I shall leave you my cottage, my spindle, my weaver's shuttle, and my needle. With these you will be able to earn your bread. Remember to always be good and kind, and you will be happy."

Soon after this the old woman died, and the girl was left to live all alone. Every day she worked at her spinning, weaving, and sewing, and she managed to get by. As soon as she finished any work, someone was sure to buy it. But she remained quite poor.

Now about this time a prince was traveling through the countryside in search of a bride. He could not marry a poor woman, and he did not wish for a rich one. "My bride must be both the poorest and the richest," he said as he traveled from town to town.

Soon he came to the town where the young maid lived, and he asked, "Who here is the richest maiden?" He was told that the richest maiden lived in a large mansion near the town square. So the prince went there and found her sitting outside her splendid house, dressed in the most beautiful clothes. When he rode by, the maiden curtsied gracefully and smiled. She hoped the prince would choose her. The prince looked at her, but he said nothing and rode on.

Next he asked "Who here is the poorest maiden in the town?" He was told she was the young girl who spun, wove, and sewed all day. So the prince

rode to her cottage and found the young
woman working at her sewing. As the prince
watched her through the window, the girl looked
up and saw him, then at once she blushed and
turned away. She began to spin and did not look up
again until the prince turned to leave. Then the
young maid said, ''How hot it is!'' and went to the
window, where she watched the prince ride into the
distance. She did not leave the window until all she could
see was the fine white feather in the prince's hat.

Then she went back to work and began to sing:

> ''Spindle, spindle, go and see,
> And bring my true love back to me.''

As she finished her song the spindle jumped from her hand and flew out
of the room. The girl watched it dance merrily down the road, trailing a
golden thread behind it. It soon vanished from sight.

Since the maiden now had no spindle, she began to weave. Meanwhile,
the spindle continued down the road and ran out of thread just as it reached
the prince. ''What is this?'' he said. ''I will follow the golden thread and see
where it leads me.''

In her cottage as the girl sat weaving, she again began to sing:

> ''Shuttle, weave both weft and woof,
> Bring my love beneath my roof.''

The shuttle instantly leaped from her hand and sprang out the door. On
the threshold of the cottage it began to weave the most beautiful carpet ever
seen. When the carpet was finished, it showed a brightly colored pattern of
fine flowers, rabbits, and deer, and birds with feathers so real that it seemed
possible that the birds might sing.

Now the poor girl had no shuttle, so she began to sew. This time she sang:

"Needle, needle, stitch away,
Make my chamber bright and gay."

This time the needle fell from her hand and danced around the room too fast to see. It was as if invisible spirits were working at the needle's command, for soon the chairs and tables were covered with the richest fabrics imaginable, and beautiful drapes hung on the windows. Just as the needle finished its work the girl saw the prince being led back to her cottage by the spindle and the golden thread.

When the prince arrived at the gate, he got off his horse and walked over the magnificent carpet and into the cottage. The young maiden blushed like a rose, and the prince thought she was more beautiful than anyone he had ever seen. "Here is a maiden both poor and rich," thought the prince, and he immediately asked her to be his bride.

The girl happily said yes. So the prince placed her on his horse and led her back to his palace. There they celebrated with the most beautiful wedding anyone had ever seen, and the entire kingdom rejoiced for a month.

Of course the girl had brought her spindle, her shuttle, and her needle along with her. They were placed in the palace with all the kingdom's richest treasures, and were carefully guarded forever after.

Hansel and Gretel

Once upon a time in a dark wood there lived an old woodsman with his wife and their two small children, Hansel and Gretel. Although he was poor, the woodsman had always earned enough to feed his family, until one year a great famine swept through the land. Day by day the poor woodsman and his family had less and less to eat, until at last they had almost nothing at all.

"I don't know what will happen to us," the poor man said to his wife one night as they lay in bed. "We have bread for tomorrow and after that we will have no more food."

"There is only one solution," said the wife. "Tomorrow morning we will take the children to the thickest part of the forest. There we will build a big fire and give each of them a piece of bread. We will tell them that we will fetch them after we have finished our work. But we will leave them there. They will never find their way home and we shall be rid of them forever."

"No!" said the husband. "I cannot leave my children alone in the woods. Wild beasts may kill them!"

"You fool," said the wife, who did not love Hansel and Gretel as much as their father did. "If you do not, we shall all four die of hunger. You might as well start making our coffins." The wife nagged and nagged her husband, and finally he agreed to the wife's plan.

The children, who were too hungry to fall asleep, heard all that their parents said. Gretel said to her brother, ''How terrible this is! I hope tomorrow never comes,'' and she began to cry.

But Hansel consoled her and told her not to worry. ''Somehow, dear Gretel, we'll manage to find a way to escape from the forest.''

Hansel lay quietly until he was sure his parents had fallen asleep. When all was still, Hansel slipped out of the house, and in the clear moonlight he noticed that the white pebbles that lay around the house glistened like tiny bits of silver. This gave him an idea. He quickly collected as many pebbles as he could and hid them in his coat pockets. Then he crept back to bed.

''Well, little Gretel,'' said her brother, ''God will not desert us tomorrow.'' Then they both fell asleep.

Before the sun was up the next morning, the woodsman and his wife woke the children.

''Get dressed, you lazy children,'' she said. ''We're going to fetch wood deep in the forest.'' Then she gave each of them a crust of bread, and said, ''Save this for your lunch, because there is no more.''

The family set out for the woods. As they walked farther and farther into the thick forest, Hansel kept stopping to look back.

''Why do you look back so often?'' asked his father.

''I was watching a white kitten sitting on the roof waving farewell,'' said Hansel.

His mother said, ''Stupid child! That is not a kitten—it is only the sun shining off the chimney.''

But Hansel had not really been watching a kitten. Each time, he had stopped to carefully drop one of the little white pebbles onto the path.

When they were deep in the forest, the children's father said, ''I will build a big fire so that you will keep warm while your mother and I go and chop wood.''

So the woodsman built a fire, and when it was nice and hot, their mother said, ''Lie down and rest. After our work is done we will come to take you home.''

Hansel and Gretel huddled together, and when lunchtime came, they ate their bread. All day long they could hear the sound of an axe nearby. They thought that this was their father working, but they were wrong. Their mother had tied a dead branch to a tree, and as the wind blew, the branch

banged against it. Their parents were really at home without them. The children sat by the fire for a long time, and finally fell asleep. When they awoke, it was nighttime, the fire had gone out, and the forest was very dark. Gretel began to cry. Her big brother comforted her.

"Do not worry," he said. "When the moon comes up we are sure to find our way home. I have dropped white pebbles along the path that will lead us back."

When the moon rose, Hansel took Gretel's hand and led the way. It was easy to follow the path because the pebbles shone in the moonlight like little bits of silver. They walked and walked, and by morning they were home.

"Terrible children," said their mother when she saw them, "staying out in the woods so late." But their father was truly happy to see them, and hugged them both close.

It wasn't long after this that there was a second great famine. Once again the children overheard their mother tell their father that they must be abandoned.

"This time," she said, "we will take them so deep into the woods that they will never be able to escape. Either the children die or we die."

"No!" said their father. "We must share even our very last scrap of bread with Hansel and Gretel." But the wife argued and argued, and knowing that her husband had given in the first time, she knew he would do so again. And finally he did.

As soon as their parents were asleep, Hansel got out of bed to go again and collect the pebbles that would guide their way home. But this time the mother had barred the door, and Hansel could not get out.

"We will surely perish in the dark forest," cried Gretel.

"Sleep, little sister," said Hansel. "God will surely help us."

Early the next morning, the mother woke her children. As before, she gave both of them a crust of bread for their lunch. On the way into the forest, Hansel stopped every few yards to drop a small piece of his bread along the path.

"Why do you look back again and again?" asked his father.

"I was looking at a pigeon on the roof of the house waving farewell to us," he said.

His mother said, "Stupid child! That is not a pigeon—it is only the sun shining off the chimney." But Hansel continued to stop and carefully drop the little breadcrumbs.

When they arrived in the thickest part of the forest, their father built a large fire, and their mother told them to stay by it while she and her husband went to cut wood. Again Hansel and Gretel were told that their parents would be back for them in the evening. They stayed close by the fire, and at lunchtime they shared Gretel's piece of bread between them. As it grew dark there was no sign of their parents anywhere, and Gretel began to cry. Hansel comforted her.

"When the moon rises we shall be able to find our way," he said. "I have left breadcrumbs along the path to guide us home." But when the moon came out the children could find no trace of the breadcrumbs, for the birds and little animals that scamper in the forest had eaten them all. Hansel took Gretel's hand and said to her, "Do not worry, dear sister. We will find our way somehow." But though the children wandered that whole night long and the following day too, they could not find their way home. The more they wandered, the deeper into the forest they walked, and the more tired and hungry they became. They had nothing to eat but a few wild berries which they found here and there.

After wandering in the woods for three whole days, they happened to see a snow-white bird singing on a branch. The bird's song was so sweet that the children stopped to listen. When the bird finished his song, he gracefully flew away, and the children ran after him. The bird landed on the roof of a pretty little cottage. As the children drew near to the cottage they saw that it was made entirely of beautiful things to eat: the walls were sweet breads and the roof was made of all sorts of cake. The windows were delicious transparent sugar.

"At last we can eat something," said Hansel as he broke off a piece of the roof and happily started eating. Gretel began to eat parts of the windows. But no sooner had they started eating than a hissing voice called out from the house:

"Nibble, nibble, little mouse,
 Who's that nibbling on my house?"

Suddenly the cottage door opened, and out hobbled an old, old woman leaning on a stick. Hansel and Gretel were very frightened, but the woman just smiled a crooked smile and said, "Have no fear, little children. I'm glad the bird led you here. Come in and stay with me. Nothing bad will happen to you." She took them inside and prepared a delicious meal of sugared

pancakes with apples and nuts and creamy milk to drink. "Eat," she said, "for I know you are hungry." When they had eaten their fill, she prepared two little beds for them and invited them to sleep.

The old woman was only pretending to be kind—she was really an old witch who had built her house of sweet things especially to entrap children. Whenever she managed to capture any children, she killed them, cooked them, and happily ate them up. And that is exactly what she planned to do with Hansel and Gretel.

Very early the next morning, the witch went to the children's beds. She watched them as they lay happily sleeping and said to herself, "What fine meals they will make." Then she picked Hansel up in her shriveled old arms and carried him to her stable, where she locked him in an iron cage. When Hansel woke up, he was very frightened and shouted to be let out, but the witch paid no attention.

Then she went and woke up Gretel and yelled, "Get up, you lazy child, there's work to do. You must start cooking for your brother, so that he will get fat and make a nice meal for me." Gretel started to cry, but the wicked old witch only laughed.

So it was that every morning Gretel had to cook fine food for Hansel, but she herself was fed only crab shells. And every morning after Hansel had eaten, the witch, whose eyesight was not very good, went to the stable and said, "Stick your finger between the bars so that I may feel if you are fat and ready to eat." But Hansel fooled her by sticking out a tiny bone he had found. The witch could not understand why Hansel was not getting fatter. Finally, after four weeks, she became angry and impatient, and said, "Even though you are still thin, I will eat you tomorrow."

The next morning the witch made Gretel hang a large cauldron of water over the big fire in the kitchen. Then she said, "First we'll bake the dough. I have already heated up the oven, but I don't know if it's hot enough." She pushed Gretel toward the oven, where the flames were jumping up. "Crawl into the oven," said the witch, "and tell me if it's ready." The witch planned to shut the oven door once Gretel was inside, and bake her and eat her for lunch along with her brother. But Gretel was too clever. She knew what the witch was planning.

"I don't know how to get in," she said. "Show me."

"Stupid child," said the witch. And she leaned into the oven. Gretel gave her a big push. Then she slammed the oven door shut and fastened the bolt. The witch began to howl, but Gretel did not listen. She ran out of the house to the stable and freed Hansel from his cage.

"The wicked witch is dead. We are free," said Gretel. Hansel and Gretel hugged and kissed each other and danced around the stable.

Later they found chests full of gems of every kind and color, as well as pearls and coins of gold and silver in the house. They gathered as much as they could into their pockets, then left the witch's house to find their parents.

Hansel and Gretel walked for many hours until the forest became familiar, and at last they saw their parents' house in the distance. They ran inside and threw their arms around their father's neck and showered him with kisses. He had been miserable ever since he had left them in the forest, and had missed them more than ever since his wife had died. The children emptied their pockets and showed their father all they had found. Then they told their father all about the witch. First they cried, but then they laughed and were all happy together, not just on that day but forever after.

Rumpelstiltskin

nce upon a time there was a poor miller who had little enough to eat, but a most beautiful daughter. One day he went to see the king, and to make himself seem important he said, "Not only is my daughter beautiful, but she can sit at her spinning wheel and spin straw into gold." The king, who had seen and heard much, was very eager to see this and told the miller to bring his daughter to the castle the very next day.

The following morning the girl was brought before the king, who immediately took her to a room filled with straw. In the far corner was a spinning wheel. "With this spinning wheel," said the king, "you must spin all this straw into gold. If this is not done by early tomorrow morning, you must die." Then he left her and locked the door. The poor girl did not know how to spin straw into gold, and she was very frightened to be left all alone. She began to cry bitterly, for she was sure that in the morning she would die.

Just then, an ugly little man popped through the window. "Why are you crying?" he asked. "I must spin all of this straw into gold and I don't know how it is to be done," the girl replied, sobbing. "What will you give me if I do this for you?" the little man asked. "My necklace," offered the girl.

So the little man took her necklace, sat down in front of the wheel, and began to spin. Whirr, whirr, whirr, three times the wheel went round and the spool was full. Whirr, whirr, whirr and another spool was full and so it went until the night had passed and all the straw was gleaming gold. The girl was delighted. The little man laughed, then leaped merrily out the window and disappeared.

When the king returned and saw the gold, he became very excited. "I want more gold!" he exclaimed greedily. He then led the girl to another room with even more straw than the first. "Now," he said, "you must turn all of *this* into gold too. If you do not, I have told you already what will happen." When the king left her, the girl again began to cry. Suddenly the little man popped through the window. "What will you give me this time,"

he asked, "if I spin this straw into gold for you?"

"I will give you my little ring," said the girl. So the little man took the ring, slipped it on his finger, and began to spin. When morning came, all the straw was gold, and with his work finished, the little man again disappeared.

This time the king was even more excited, but he still was not satisfied, and wanted even more gold. So he took the miller's daughter to yet another room, which was larger than either of the two she had been in, and where there was more straw than she had ever seen. "Spin this straw into gold," said the king. "If you can do this, I will marry you and you will sit beside me as my queen. Although you are only a poor miller's daughter, I could not find a richer wife in all the world. But if you cannot spin this straw into gold, you must die."

The king had barely locked the door when—*pop!*—through the window came the little man. "What will you give me if I help you this time?" he asked. "I have nothing left to give," the poor girl cried sadly. "Promise me," said the little man, "that when you become queen you will give me your first-born child."

The girl thought to herself: "I must have the straw spun to gold by tomorrow morning or I will die. And I do not know if the king will truly marry me." So she promised to give the little man what he asked for, and he set to work at once. All night long he sat and spun, until at last all the straw was gold. Then he disappeared just as mysteriously as he had arrived.

When the king came early the next day, he was happier than ever. A room full of gold! He gladly kept his promise and married the miller's beautiful daughter.

After a year had passed, the queen gave birth to a child. One night when she was all alone in her room, the little man suddenly popped through the window and said: "You must now keep your promise and give me your child." The queen, who had forgotten all about the old man, could not bear to lose her child and began to weep. "I will give you anything in my kingdom," she said, "if only I can keep my child."

"No," he said. "A child is the greatest treasure in all the world, and nothing else will do."

The queen cried as though her heart would break, and at last the little man took pity on her. "I will give you three days to guess what my name is," he said. "If within three days you guess correctly, I will let you keep your child."

The queen thought long and hard of all the names she knew and she sent

a messenger to scour the country to find names she did not know. When the little man came the next day, she asked him: "Is your name Thomas?" He shook his head. "That is not my name," he said. "Is your name Lawrence?" He shook his head. "Is your name Kaspar, Melchior, Belshazzar?" And she listed all the other names she knew, one after the other, but to each he shook his head and answered, "That is not my name." The next day the queen again sent messengers all over the kingdom to find still other names, no matter how unusual. When the little man returned the second night, she tried every new name, even the strangest and funniest. "Is your name Sheepshank, Peaseblossom, Nicklenose, or Brink?" she asked. But for each name the little man shook his head and answered, "That is not my name."

On the third day the queen could think of no other names and began to despair. She was about to give up when a messenger came running into the palace and told the queen: "As I was walking in the woods this morning, I saw a little old man dancing on a grassy knoll, singing this song:

'To these woods all dark and wild,
I shall bring the queen's sweet child.
It shall all work very well,
If my name I never tell.
Rumpelstiltskin, yes, oh yes,
Is a name she'll never guess.'''

The queen was delighted. She felt sure that now she knew the little man's name. When he returned again that night, he said, "My queen, now you must tell me my name or give me your first-born child. What is my name?"

"Is it Bardolph?" she asked. He shook his head. "That is not my name," he said. "Is it Nym?" asked the queen. Again he shook his head. "That is not my name," he replied.

"Could it be—Rumpelstiltskin?"

The little man was so surprised and angry that he shouted, "The devil has told you my name!" With that he stamped his right foot with such force that his whole leg sank into the ground up to his waist. Then he grabbed his left foot with both hands, tore himself in two, and disappeared.

Snow White

Once upon a time, as the winter snow was falling, a young queen sat at a window framed in the blackest ebony. As she sewed she pricked her thumb, and a drop of red blood fell on the white snow. "Oh!" she thought. "How I would like to have a child with skin as white as snow, lips as red as blood, and hair as black as ebony."

Her wish soon came true, for not long after, she gave birth to a beautiful baby daughter, whom she named Snow White. After the birth, the queen died.

The king mourned the death of his queen, but after a year he remarried. The new queen was very beautiful, but she was so proud and jealous that she could not bear the thought that anyone should be a rival to her beauty. She had an ancient magic mirror, and often she would stand in front of it, gazing at her reflection, and ask:

"Mirror, mirror, on the wall,
Who's the fairest one of all?"

And the mirror would always answer:

"My Royal Queen, I shall speak true,
There is no fairer one than you."

This made the queen happy, for the mirror always spoke the truth. But as Snow White grew she became prettier each day, until she was more beautiful than her stepmother, the queen. One day the queen asked:

"Mirror, mirror, on the wall,
Who's the fairest one of all?"

And the mirror answered:

"My Royal Queen, I shall speak true,
Snow White is fairer far than you."

The queen was greatly angered by this. Her jealousy of Snow White's beauty turned to hatred, which grew greater with each passing day, until at last she decided that Snow White must die. So the queen called her most faithful huntsman and said, "Take Snow White into the woods and kill her. Bring me back her lungs and liver."

The huntsman did as he was ordered and took Snow White deep into the woods. But when he drew his dagger, she cried, "Oh, please, huntsman, spare my life. I will run into the woods and never come back!"

Because she was so pretty, he felt sorry for Snow White and said, "Go, run away." The huntsman was sure wild beasts would soon do his job for him. Then he killed a wild boar and took its lungs and liver to the queen, who was delighted to think that Snow White was now dead.

Meanwhile Snow White ran through the dark forest, frightened by all the scary shadows. Bushes and brambles tugged at her clothes, but the wild beasts did her no harm. Finally, Snow White came to a small house. She knocked at the door, but there was no answer. So she stepped inside. Everything was neat and tidy, but all the furniture was very small. There was a little table set with seven little plates, seven little forks and knives, and seven little mugs. And at each place was a little chair, and against the wall were seven little beds.

Snow White was hungry, so she ate a small piece of bread from each plate and drank a drop of wine from each mug, so as not to use up one portion alone. She now felt tired and decided to lie down. The first bed she lay on was so small that she couldn't fit on it. She tried each bed in turn, but only the last one was large enough for her. Then she said her prayers and fell asleep.

When it was dark, the owners returned. They were seven dwarfs who dug for silver and gold deep in the mountains. As soon as they lit their seven little lamps they saw that things were not as they had left them.

The first said: "Who has been sitting in my chair?"

The second said: "Who has been eating my bread?"

The third said: "Who has been drinking from my mug?"

The fourth said: "Who has been eating from my plate?"

The fifth said: "Who has been using my fork?"

The sixth said: "Who has been using my knife?"

But the seventh dwarf saw Snow White, and he quickly called to the others, and said, "Look, someone is lying in my bed!"

"How beautiful she is," they all whispered. The seven dwarfs didn't want to wake her, so they quietly ate their supper and went to bed. The seventh dwarf slept one hour with each of his companions, so he managed to pass the night without missing his own bed.

When Snow White awoke in the morning, the dwarfs were already awake. She was very frightened to find seven little men looking at her. But the dwarfs spoke kindly to her and asked her name.

"I am Snow White," she told them.

"How did you come to our house?" they asked. She told the dwarfs about her cruel stepmother, and how she had run through the woods until she found their house.

"Dear Snow White," they said, "please stay with us. We will be happy to have you here always."

"Yes," said Snow White, "I will be happy to stay with you."

So every day, the dwarfs went to work in their mine, and Snow White cared for the house and made their supper. They were happy together, except

it worried the dwarfs that Snow White was alone all day.

"When we are away, don't let anyone into the house," they warned her. "If your stepmother learns that you are alive, she will find you."

Not long after the huntsman returned to the palace, the wicked queen asked her mirror:

"Mirror, mirror, on the wall,
Who's the fairest one of all?"

And the mirror replied:

"My Royal Queen, I shall speak true,
Snow White is fairer far than you.
Deep in the woods she does now dwell,
With seven dwarfs who love her well."

You can imagine how angry the queen became! She now knew that the huntsman had deceived her. So she devised an evil plan. The queen dressed up as an old peddler woman and went to the house of the seven dwarfs. She knocked at their door and cried out: "Pretty laces! Pretty ribbons! Buy my pretty lace!" Snow White did not recognize the queen, and so she let her in.

"How nice you will look in my pretty laces!" said the queen. "Try them!" Snow White let the queen lace her up. But the queen pulled the laces so tightly that Snow White dropped down as if dead.

"You're not so pretty!" laughed the wicked woman, hurrying away.

When the dwarfs came home, how frightened they were to see their poor, dear Snow White! They saw how tightly she had been laced and cut all the laces. Slowly Snow White began to come back to life. When she told them what had happened, they knew it was the wicked queen who had tricked Snow White, and they said, "Be sure never to let anyone in again." When the queen arrived home, she quickly went and asked the mirror:

"Mirror, mirror, on the wall,
Who's the fairest one of all?"

Again the mirror replied:

"My Royal Queen, I shall speak true,
Snow White is fairer far than you.
Deep in the woods she does now dwell,
With seven dwarfs who love her well."

When the queen heard this, she became pale with anger. "I must think of a way to finish Snow White forever!" she screamed.

The queen decided to make a poison, into which she dipped a comb. Then she disguised herself as a different peddler woman and again went to the house of the seven dwarfs. "Buy my pretty trinkets!" she cried.

Snow White longed to look at the trinkets, but she remembered the dwarfs' warning, and said: "Go away, for I cannot let anyone in."

"At least look at this pretty comb," the peddler woman said, holding it up to the window. The comb was so beautiful that Snow White could not resist and let the old woman in.

"Now," said the wicked queen, "let me comb your beautiful hair." But no sooner had the comb touched Snow White's hair than she dropped down as if dead. The queen laughed cruelly as she fled from the house.

That evening when the dwarfs returned they were again struck with horror. They knew Snow White's wicked stepmother had returned, and they searched Snow White until they found the poison comb. They pulled it from her hair, and slowly she began to awaken. This time she made a solemn promise to never again let anyone into the house.

As soon as the queen arrived home she ran to her mirror and shouted:

"Mirror, mirror, on the wall,
Who's the fairest one of all?"

And the mirror replied:

"My Royal Queen, I shall speak true,
Snow White is fairer far than you.
Deep in the woods she does now dwell,
With seven dwarfs who love her well."

The queen trembled and screamed in her rage. "This time I shall certainly kill Snow White. She shall never awaken!" Then she went to a secret chamber, and there with the blackest of black magic she made a poison apple. It was the most beautiful red apple, but just one tiny bite from it would mean certain death. This time she disguised herself as an old farm woman, and again she went and knocked at their door.

"I cannot open the door," said Snow White, "for I have promised the dear dwarfs to let no one in."

"Well," said the queen, "I do not ask to come in. I ask you only to buy my apples. Try one bite from this delicious apple. Here, I will cut it in half, and we shall share it. Isn't it beautiful?" Only one side of the apple was poisonous, and that side she held out to Snow White. It did look delicious!

"All right," said Snow White. "I will have one bite." But as soon as she bit it she dropped down dead. The queen laughed, for she was sure the poison was so strong that the dwarfs could never bring Snow White back to life. She ran all the way back to her castle, and as soon as she arrived she went at once to her mirror and said:

> "Mirror, mirror, on the wall,
>   Who's the fairest one of all?"

The mirror replied:

> "My Royal Queen, I shall speak true,
>   There is no fairer one than you."

When the dwarfs came home, they knew that the queen had again been at the house. They lifted Snow White and searched for something poisonous. Then they cut all her laces, and they looked in her hair for a comb. But the dwarfs found nothing. They did not know what had killed their beautiful Snow White. They gently put Snow White on her bed, placed flowers in her hair, and for three whole days they did nothing but weep. They missed her so! When it came time to bury her they saw that her beauty was unchanged: Death seemed only to have put her gently to sleep.

"We cannot put her in the cold, black ground," said the dwarfs. "We will make her a beautiful glass coffin." And when the coffin was finished they wrote on the lid, in golden letters:

HERE LIES A ROYAL PRINCESS.

They put the coffin on the highest peak of a beautiful mountain, and one dwarf was always there to keep watch over it.

Time went by, but inside the glass coffin Snow White always looked the same: her skin as white as snow, her lips and cheeks as red as blood, her hair as black as ebony.

Now one day a prince happened to come to the mountaintop where Snow White lay. He was struck by her beauty.

"Please tell me," he said to the dwarfs, "who is this fair princess? I will give anything if you will let me have her coffin."

"We are sorry," said the dwarfs, "but we would not part with it for all the gold in the world. Snow White was our dearest friend."

"Please," begged the prince, "I cannot live without your princess. I will watch over her coffin always, and it will be the most cherished possession in my kingdom."

The prince seemed so in love and so sad that at last the dwarfs felt sorry for him. They told him he could have the coffin. As his servants carried it down the mountain they stumbled, and the piece of poison apple fell from Snow White's mouth. She opened her eyes and asked, "Where am I?"

The prince told her all that had happened and then said: "I love you. Will you marry me and come to live in my castle?"

Snow White happily agreed, and together the prince and princess rode away to their kingdom. They planned a splendid wedding, and to this feast was invited Snow White's stepmother. When the wicked queen was dressed in her fancy clothes, she asked her mirror once again:

> "Mirror, mirror, on the wall,
>   Who's the fairest one of all?"

And the mirror answered:

> "My Royal Queen, I shall speak true,
>   Snow White is fairer far than you."

These words made the queen angrier than ever, but she went to the wedding. But when she saw Snow White so radiantly beautiful in her white wedding gown, the queen became so angry that she dropped dead.

Snow White and her prince were married that very day, and from then on lived happily ever after.

The Wolf and the Seven Little Kids

Once upon a time there was an old mother goat who had seven pretty little children whom she loved very much. One day, before going to the forest to get them food, she called her children to her. "My dears," she said, "I must go to the forest for food. I must leave you alone. Be on your guard for the wolf. He may come to the house to eat you up. He will try to disguise himself, so that you will let him in. But you can tell if it's the wolf by his black feet and rough voice. Do not let him in."

"Don't worry, Mother dear," said the children. "We will be careful." So the mother goat kissed each child good-bye and went happily on her way.

Not long after the mother goat had left, there was a knock on the door.

"Open the door, sweet children," said a voice. "Your mother has come home with delicious treats for all." This voice was rough and the smart children remembered their mother's warning. They knew it was the wolf.

"Go away, wolf!" cried the children. "We know you are not our dear mother. She has a gentle voice, and your voice is rough."

So the wolf went into town and bought himself a large sack of chalk. This he swallowed and soon his voice softened.

Back he went to the goats' house and knocked again on the door. "Open the door, sweet children. Your mother has come home with delicious treats for all," the wolf said in his softest voice. But the wolf had put his big black paws on the window sill, and the children saw them.

"Go away, wolf!" cried the children. "You are not our dear mother. She has pretty little white feet and you have big black ugly ones. You are the wolf!"

So the wolf ran back to town once more. There he found a baker and told him, "Put some flour on my feet because they itch and burn." The baker did as the wolf asked. Next the wolf said to the baker, "Throw some white meal over them too."

The baker thought to himself: "The wolf needs a disguise. He is up to no good." So he said, "No, I will not give you any white meal."

This made the wolf very angry. "Either you give it to me or I'll eat you up," he growled. The baker quickly gave the wolf the meal.

Now the wolf went for the third time to the goats' house, and for the third time knocked on the door and said, "Open the door, sweet children.

Your mother has come home with delicious treats for all."

"Show us your paws," called the children, "so we can tell if you are truly our dear mother."

Through the window the wolf showed his white paws and the children were fooled. Happily they opened the door. In sprang the wolf! "Help!" cried the children as they ran to hide.

Each child quickly found a different hiding place—the first under the table, the second in a bed, the third behind the stove, the fourth in a kitchen corner, the fifth in a cupboard, the sixth under a wash bowl, and the seventh in the clock case. But one by one the wolf found them and gulped them down hungrily. Only the youngest child, the one who was hiding in the clock case, was not found. Now the wolf, having eaten six children and satisfied his appetite, went out into the meadow and fell asleep under a tree.

It wasn't much later when the old mother goat returned home, and seeing the cottage door open and the house in a terrible mess with pillows and quilts and chairs all out of place, she knew at once that the wolf had come. One by one she called for her children and heard nothing in reply. When she got to the last name, the name of her youngest child, she heard a tiny, soft cry. "Help me, dear Mother. I am in the clock case." She ran and got the child from the case, and learned all that had happened. Oh, how she cried when he told her that his sisters and brothers had all been eaten up!

The mother and the youngest child went out into the meadow to get some fresh air. There, under a big tree, they saw the wolf sleeping. He was snoring so loudly that all the branches shook on the tree. As the mother goat looked at him, she noticed that something was moving in the wolf's belly.

"Good heavens!" exclaimed the mother goat. "Perhaps my children are alive in the wolf's stomach! Perhaps in his greed he swallowed them whole!"

She quickly sent the youngest child running home to get a scissors, a needle, and some thread. When the child returned, his mother quickly cut open the wolf's stomach. And there she saw the head of one of her children! He sprang out of the wolf's stomach, and as the mother goat cut further, out sprang another child, and another and another, until all six children were free.

None of the children were hurt because the wolf had indeed eaten them too fast to even chew.

How happy they all were! They hugged and kissed one another, and their mother cried for joy.

Suddenly the mother goat had an idea. "Quickly, children, go and fetch some big rocks. We will put them in the wolf's stomach while he is still asleep." So the children ran and brought back the biggest rocks they could carry and put as many into the wolf's stomach as they could fit. Before the wolf woke up, the mother goat sewed his stomach closed.

Later, when the wolf had finished his nap, he felt very thirsty and went to the well for some water. As he walked the rocks knocked against one another, and he said:

> "What, oh what, is in my gut?
> I just ate six children, but
> They would never make such knocks;
> Is my belly full of rocks?"

He leaned over to drink from the well. But the rocks were so heavy that he fell in and was drowned. The seven children saw him fall and ran happily to tell their mother. She made a nice lunch to celebrate the end of the mean wolf, and invited the baker from town to join them.

The Golden Goose

Once in a distant land there lived a man who had three sons. The youngest was named Dullhead because he was considered very dull and stupid. Everyone, even his family, laughed at him and teased him and treated him unkindly.

One day the eldest son of the family had to go into the forest to cut wood. Before he left, his mother packed some rich cake and fine wine in a basket for him to take as refreshment.

He had not traveled far when he met a little old gray-haired man. "Good day," said the old man. "I am thirsty and hungry. Would you please share a little of your food with me?"

The eldest son replied, "If I give you some of my cake and fine wine there will be less for me when I am hungry and thirsty. I'm clever enough to know this. Go away and leave me alone." And with that, the boy turned and continued his journey into the forest. Not long after the eldest son had started cutting wood his axe slipped and he cut his arm badly. So serious was the wound that he was forced to leave his chopping and go home to have his arm bound up.

Now it was the second brother's turn to go to the forest to cut wood. As

she had done for her eldest son, the mother packed a basket of rich cake and fine wine for her second son. As the young man traveled through the forest, he too met the little old gray-haired man. "Please," said the man, "I am thirsty and hungry. Will you share your cake and wine with me?"

But like the first son, the second spoke harshly. "Leave me alone, you silly old man. Do you think I am too stupid to know that if I give you some of my food and drink I will have less left for me? Be off." And with this he went one way, leaving the old man to go another. Soon after the second son started cutting wood, he too was punished for his selfishness. He accidentally struck his leg with his axe and had to be carried home at once.

Now Dullhead asked his father: "Please may I go to the forest and cut wood? We need some and my two brothers cannot do it."

"Certainly not," said his father. "Both your good brothers have cut themselves. You, Dullhead, can do no better than they. You know nothing about using an axe."

But Dullhead begged and begged, and at last his father agreed. "Go, then," he said. "Perhaps you will learn from your mistake, once you too have hurt yourself." This time the mother packed only an old piece of cake baked in the cinders and a bottle of sour beer in the basket that she handed to Dullhead.

When Dullhead arrived in the forest, he too met the little old gray-haired man. "Please," said the man, "share some of your cake and your drink. I am thirsty and hungry."

Dullhead replied, "I have only stale cinder-cake and sour beer. It is not much, but I will gladly share with you."

So they sat down together to share what little food that they had. But when Dullhead unwrapped his old cake, he found it had magically turned to fresh rich cake and that the sour beer had turned to fine wine. When they had finished eating the old man said cheerfully, "You have been kind to share what you had with me. For this I will bring you luck. Over there is an old tree. If you cut it down, you will find something magical hidden at its roots." Then the old man disappeared among the trees.

At once, Dullhead started cutting down the tree the man had pointed to. When he finally got to the stump he found a goose whose feathers were pure gold. He picked up the glittering goose and took it with him to an inn, where he decided to stay the night.

The innkeeper had three daughters, and each one was filled with curiosity as to what sort of goose would have beautiful gold feathers. Each daughter decided that she would like a feather of her own, and thought she would have no difficulty in getting Dullhead to leave the goose for a moment, so that she might pluck just one feather.

It wasn't long before this happened. As soon as Dullhead left the goose alone, the eldest daughter quickly tried to grab a feather. But the moment her hand touched the goose it instantly stuck fast, and she could not get it free.

Only a moment later the second daughter came in, and seeing that Dullhead was gone, she too went to pluck a feather. But when she touched the goose, her hand also stuck fast to the bird. Just then the youngest daughter came in. As she came near the goose the two older sisters cried, "Stay away! Stay away! Don't touch the goose!" But the youngest sister ignored them. She wanted her chance to get a feather, so she too stuck fast to the goose. The three young women pulled this way and that to get free, but nothing worked, and they unhappily spent the night stuck to the golden goose.

The next morning Dullhead set off with his goose, not worrying about the three sisters who were still attached to it. Dullhead walked with his goose tucked carefully under his arm, and the sisters trailed along behind him. They had to run in order to keep up with him. The group had not gone far when they met a parson. "For shame," he said. "Three girls running after a boy! This is not right! Leave the boy alone!" But no sooner had the parson tried to pull the girls away, than he too became stuck and had to run along with them.

Next a clerk came by, and seeing the parson running after the girls, who were running after Dullhead, said, "Parson, you have no time for running around—we have a christening today." But as the clerk reached out to pull the parson away he too became stuck. Now there were five people running along one after another all stuck together and all trying to keep up with Dullhead and his goose.

Soon they passed two peasants, and the parson called to them, "Please pull me and the clerk free. We are stuck to these girls!" So the peasants came running, but no sooner had they touched the clerk than they too became

stuck. And so the procession trailing Dullhead and his golden goose became even longer.

Before long this procession arrived in a town where there lived a king with a daughter so serious that no one had ever been able to make her laugh. No one could even make her smile! The king wanted nothing more than to make his daughter happy, and had declared that if any man could make her laugh he would have the princess for his wife.

Dullhead went straight to the princess with his beautiful golden goose tucked under his arm and the seven people attached behind in a wild procession running and twisting this way and that to keep up with him. The spectacle looked so funny that the princess laughed and laughed and laughed when she saw it—in fact she laughed so much that people wondered if she would ever stop. So Dullhead went to the king and claimed the princess for his bride. But the king shook his head. He hadn't expected someone like Dullhead to win his daughter's hand. ''There is *one* more condition,'' said the king quickly, ''if you are to marry my daughter. You must first bring me

a man who can drink a whole cellar of wine.'' The king smiled to himself. He was certain there was no such man in the kingdom.

Dullhead remembered the little old gray-haired man who had helped him before, and he went back to the woods to find him. But sitting on the stump of the tree that Dullhead had cut down sat another old man. He looked very sad. ''Why do you look so unhappy?'' asked Dullhead. ''Because,'' said the old man, ''I think I will die of thirst. Water does not quench my thirst, and a whole barrel of wine has hardly helped either.''

''I think I can help you,'' said Dullhead happily.

He took the old man to the king's castle and sat him down in the cellar. There the man passed the entire day drinking barrels and barrels of wine. As night fell, he finally finished the very last drop in the very last barrel.

Dullhead went back to the king to once again claim his bride. But still the king did not like the idea of Dullhead as his son-in-law. ''There is just *one* more condition before you can marry my splendid daughter,'' he said. ''You must bring me a man who can eat a whole mountain of bread.'' The king was certain there was no such man in the kingdom.

But no sooner had the king spoken than Dullhead was on his way back to the forest. Again on the very stump of the tree he had cut down sat another old man looking weak and pulling his belt in very tightly around his waist. ''Why do you do this?'' asked Dullhead.

''I am so hungry I feel I will die,'' said the man. ''I have eaten a whole ovenful of bread and yet my belt gets looser and looser.''

Dullhead said, ''I think I can help you,'' and at once led the man to the king's palace. The king had ordered that all the flour in the kingdom be used to make an enormous mountain of bread. The old man was led to it, and stood there the whole day happily eating. When at last the sun went down, he swallowed the last little crumb of the bread mountain.

Again Dullhead went to the king for his daughter's hand. Again the king thought of another condition to keep Dullhead from having her. ''This time I want a ship that can sail on land or on water,'' he said. ''If you can satisfy this last condition, you will marry my daughter.''

So off went Dullhead to the forest, and found the little old gray-haired man who had helped him when he first went to chop wood. The man said, ''I have done many things for you and I will give you the ship you now want —all because you were thoughtful and generous and happy to share the little you had with a poor old man." And without another word, the little old man gave Dullhead the ship and then disappeared. So Dullhead took it to the king, and without further delay the king gave Dullhead his daughter.

Dullhead and the princess had a magnificent wedding, and the whole kingdom rejoiced. People now knew that Dullhead wasn't stupid at all, but smart and good and kind. Never again was he called Dullhead. And after the king died, he became king and the princess became queen. They lived long and happily and ruled over their kingdom wisely and kindly. Of course the splendid golden goose lived with them always.

Rapunzel

Many, many years ago there lived a man and his wife who longed to have a child. At last the woman found that their wish was to be granted. At the back of their house they had a window that looked onto a splendid garden filled with beautiful flowers and wonderful herbs. This garden was surrounded by a high wall, and no one dared to go into it because it belonged to a terrible old witch. One day, while the wife was looking out her window, she saw the freshest, most delicious rampion growing beyond the wall of the garden. She truly longed to eat some of the rampion. With each passing day her desire grew stronger and stronger, but because she knew she had little chance of even tasting the tiniest morsel, she felt hopeless and miserable. At last she became quite ill and her husband became alarmed.

"What ails you, dear wife?" he asked her.

"Ah, dear husband, if I cannot have some rampion from the witch's garden, I shall die!" she replied.

Now, the husband loved his wife dearly and was prepared to risk anything rather than let her die. That night, when all was very quiet, he

stealthily climbed over the garden wall and hastily plucked some rampion for his wife. She at once made a salad of it and immediately felt better. But it was so good that her desire for rampion was greater than ever. So the next night, when all was quiet, again the husband climbed over the garden wall. But when he got to the other side, he jumped back in terror, for the witch stood before him.

"How dare you steal my rampion!" she cried angrily. "You shall suffer for it!"

"Oh, please forgive me," he begged. "My wife so desired some rampion that if she did not get some she would certainly have died."

This calmed the witch a little. "If this is true," she said, "you may take as much rampion from my garden as you like. But first, for what you have already taken, you must promise to give me the child your wife will soon give birth to. You need not fear. I will look after the child like a mother."

The man could do nothing but agree. Soon after, a beautiful little girl was born. The witch immediately took her away and gave her the name Rapunzel, which is another name for rampion.

Rapunzel grew to be the most beautiful child in the world. When she turned twelve years old, the witch locked her in an old tower deep in the woods. The tower had neither stairs nor door, and so there was no way for anyone to enter or leave. High up, near the top of the tower, was a small window. Here Rapunzel would sit and sing and watch the birds and animals in the forest. When the witch wanted to get into the tower, she would call out:

> "Rapunzel, Rapunzel,
> Let down your golden hair!"

Now, Rapunzel had long beautiful hair, as fine as spun gold. Whenever she heard the witch call, Rapunzel would undo her braids, fasten her hair to a hook above the window, and let it drop to the ground. Then the witch would climb up her hair and enter the tower.

One day a prince who was riding through the woods heard Rapunzel singing. She had a beautiful voice and often sang when she was lonely. The prince followed the sound of her voice, but when he came to the tower, he saw no door and did not know how to get in. But he loved the song so much that he decided to return every day to hear it. One day, when the prince

happened to be standing near some bushes, gazing at the
tower, he saw the witch come and call out:

"Rapunzel, Rapunzel,
Let down your golden hair!"

The hair dropped to the ground, and the witch began to
climb up. The prince watched in wonder. "Is this the
strange ladder that leads to the fair voice I have heard?"
he thought. "Then I must try it." So he hid himself
behind the bushes until the witch had gone.

The next night the prince stood below the window
and called out:

"Rapunzel, Rapunzel,
Let down your golden hair!"

Down came the beautiful hair just as it had before, and
the prince quickly climbed up.

At first, Rapunzel was very frightened when, instead of the witch, the prince appeared at her window. She had never seen a man before, but the prince spoke gently to her and seemed very kind. He told her that he had heard her singing and had so loved it that he felt he could have no peace until he met her. She blushed to hear the handsome prince talk so, and soon lost her fright. The prince then asked Rapunzel to marry him and she gladly said yes.

"I will marry you," she said, "but you must help me to escape from my tower. Every day you must bring me a piece of rope, so that I can weave a long ladder. When it is finished I will climb down, and we can go to your castle."

Every night the prince brought a piece of rope. To be sure to avoid the witch, who always left the tower before dark, he never came before sunset.

One day, without thinking, Rapunzel carelessly said to the witch, "Why is it that when I let down my hair for you, it takes a long time for you to climb up, but when I let it down for the prince, he climbs up very quickly?"

"What is this I hear you say?" cried the witch. "You wicked, deceitful child. I thought I had hidden you away from the world, but now I see you have been tricking me all along."

Angrily the witch grabbed Rapunzel's beautiful golden hair and, snip-snap, cut it all off. She then took her to a desert wilderness and there left her all alone in misery and grief.

That night when the prince came he called out as he always did:

> "Rapunzel, Rapunzel,
> Let down your golden hair!"

The witch was in the tower waiting. When she heard the prince call, she tied Rapunzel's braids to the hook above the window and let the hair fall down. The prince climbed up, and instead of finding his beloved Rapunzel, was shocked to see the ugly witch.

She laughed wickedly and said to him: "You hoped to see your true love, but your pretty bird is gone. And the cat that caught her will scratch out your eyes too!"

In his despair the prince leaped from the window, and though he was not killed, the thorns among which he landed pierced his eyes. For many years the prince wandered through the woods, blind and unhappy, living only on roots and berries, and lamenting the loss of his beloved Rapunzel.

As he wandered aimlessly he at length came to the wilderness where the witch had left Rapunzel. One day he heard singing and recognized the voice of his beloved. He ran, stumbling, to find her. When at last he found Rapunzel, she knew him instantly and embraced him and cried for joy. Two of Rapunzel's tears touched the prince's eyes, and at once he could see again. The prince took Rapunzel back to his kingdom, where they were welcomed with great joy, and there they lived happily ever after.

The Bremen Town Musicians

Long ago in a distant land there lived a farmer with a donkey who had been a good work animal for many years. But the donkey was now old, and with each passing day it became harder and harder for the donkey to pull his work load. At last the master decided he would have to put an end to the animal. He could not afford to keep feeding a donkey that was too old to work.

The donkey knew what his master was thinking, so he decided to take himself off to the town of Bremen. There, he thought, he might earn his living as a musician.

He hadn't gone very far on his journey when he came upon an old dog lying by the side of the road, panting hard and looking very tired.

"What makes you pant so?" asked the donkey. "You look so tired I think you may die."

"No," said the dog, "I am only worried. My master was going to hit me very hard on the head to bring an end to me because I am old. He says he cannot afford to keep me if I can no longer be useful for his hunting. So I ran away. But how can I earn a living?"

"Come with me," said the donkey. "I too have just left my master, and for the same reason. I am going to the city to be a musician. We can go together and try our luck." The dog agreed happily, and off the two went.

A little farther along the way they saw an old cat sitting by the side of the road, looking very gloomy.

"What's the matter?" asked the donkey. "You look so sad I think you are about to die."

"That's nearly true," said the cat. "For just because I have grown old and no longer have the energy to chase mice all day, my mistress has said she will drown me. She says she cannot afford to keep me if I don't work. So I am running away. But I am worried, for I do not know how I will earn my keep."

"We are going to the city to try and make our living as musicians," said the donkey. "You can come with us. Cats are lovely night singers, and in the city you can earn a lot of money. Please say you'll come too."

The old cat gave a cheerful meow and at once joined the donkey and the dog.

Now the three had not gone far together when they passed a farmyard where a rooster was crowing unhappily from the top of a gate.

"What a sad but beautiful tune," said the donkey to the rooster. "Why are you singing such a sad song?"

"Why?" said the rooster. "How would you feel if you knew you were about to be killed! Just this morning while I was crowing, my mistress said to the cook that she thought I would make good soup for the weekend. They want to cut off my head!"

"Come with us," said the donkey. "We have all left our masters for the same reason and are going to try and earn our living as musicians in the city. Your beautiful cock-a-doodle-doo — if you sing in key — will be a great help to us. Together we can make a little four-animal band."

"What a good idea," said the rooster happily, and he joined the group at once.

The four traveled together all day, but by nightfall they were still far from Bremen, so they went into the woods to find a safe place to sleep. The donkey and the dog lay down beside a tree, and the cat climbed up into it and made herself comfortable on a leafy branch. The rooster flew to a very high branch, and there he perched. But before he went to sleep he surveyed the land around him, as he always did, to see that there was no danger in sight.

As he looked he saw a very bright light not far away. He told his companions about it.

"It must be a farmhouse," he said. "We should go there. Perhaps we can get something to eat. We may also find someplace more comfortable to sleep."

So the four set off again. They soon reached the bright light, which was coming from a house where a band of robbers lived.

Because the donkey was tallest, he peeked through the window and told the others what he saw. There was a large room with a big table in the middle, and on the table were all kinds of good things to eat. The robbers were sitting around the table laughing and eating and talking very merrily.

"This would be a very good place for us to stay," said the rooster.

"Indeed, and there is fine food to eat," said the donkey. "But first we must devise a way to get in."

"Or a way to get them out," said the dog.

"Meow," purred the cat in agreement. The four friends talked at length, and at last settled on a plan. The donkey stood on his hind legs and rested his front legs on the window. Then the dog climbed on the donkey's back, and the cat on the dog's back, and the rooster flew up to the top and roosted on the cat's head.

The donkey gave a signal, and they started to sing. Together the donkey brayed "heehaw, heehaw," the dog barked "woof-woof, woof-woof-woof," the cat mewed "meow-meow-meow," and the rooster clucked "cock-a-doodle-doo." It was a terrible noise!

At a second signal the four animal friends broke through the window and came tumbling down on the robbers. What a commotion! The robbers had been frightened when they had seen something that looked like a tall, strange monster outside their house. But when the noise started and the animals broke through the window they were terrified and ran from the house as fast as they could.

The four animals were delighted. They immediately sat down at the table and shared the feast together. After dinner, feeling warm and lucky, they each found a comfortable bed. The donkey lay down on a heap of straw in the yard; the dog stretched out on a mat behind the kitchen door; the cat curled up on the rug in front of the fire; and the rooster perched on the top of the house. They all were tired from traveling and soon were asleep.

But the robbers had been watching the house from a distance, and when they saw that all was quiet and dark in the house, they thought that whatever had frightened them must have now left. They decided the bravest should return to the house to see if it was safe.

So the bravest robber tiptoed into the kitchen, and there he lit a match to light a candle. But by the flicker of light from the match he saw a gleam from the cat's eye. He thought this was the glow from the coals in the fire, and so he held the match to them to light the fire. The cat, awakened by the match near her eyes, sprang angrily at the man's face. She hissed and scratched him and even tried to bite him. The robber was so frightened that he ran to the door, but there he tripped over the dog, who bit him on the leg. As he fled through the yard the donkey woke up and kicked him, while the rooster on the roof above them, awakened by the noise, started crowing with displeasure. The man ran as fast as he could back to the band of robbers and told them they could never again return to the house.

"It has been taken over by an evil witch who hissed at me and scratched me with her bony fingers and tried to bite me, and then somehow she beat me to the door and tried to cut off my leg with a knife. In the yard she keeps a monster who hit me with a club, and from the roof there screeches a devil whose scream would frighten anyone." All the robbers agreed never to go near the house again.

And the musician friends lived warm and safe in the house forever after, and whenever they felt like making music they sang happily together.